* Throughout the volume, the two notes in this part offer alternatives: sing the upper, lower or both as you wish.

* Only if there is a Baritone available to partner the Alto.

SA(B) choir & piano

faberYoungVoices

Smash hits for CHRISTMAS!

Merry Christmas, everybody

Do you hear what I hear?

The Virgin Mary had a baby boy

Arranged by Robert Winter
and Gwyn Arch

faberYoungVoices

FABER **ff** MUSIC

Merry Christmas, everybody

Words and Music by
Neville Holder and James Lea
Arr. by Gwyn Arch

Do you hear what I hear?

Words and Music by
Noel Regney and Gloria Shayne
Arr. by Robert Winter

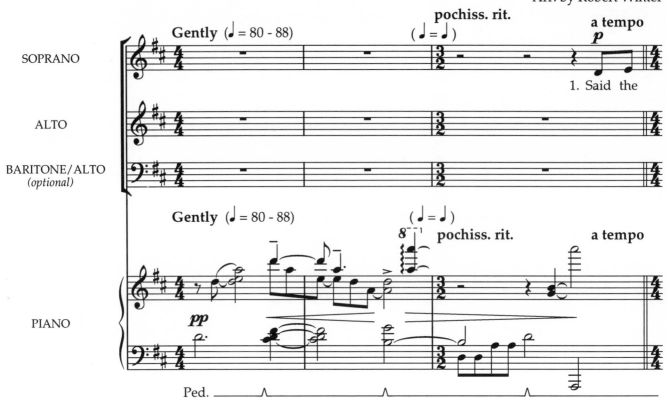

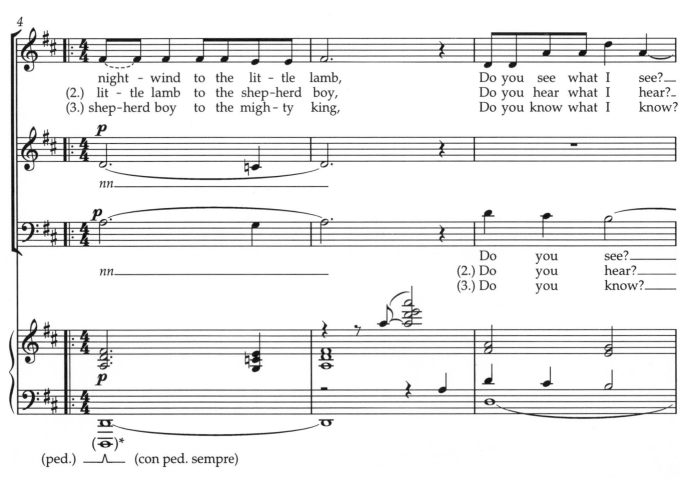

(ped.) ⌃ (con ped. sempre)

* Low D in v. 1 only

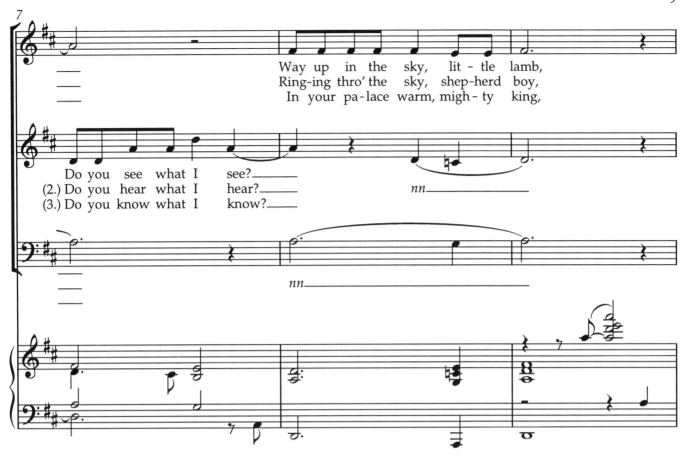

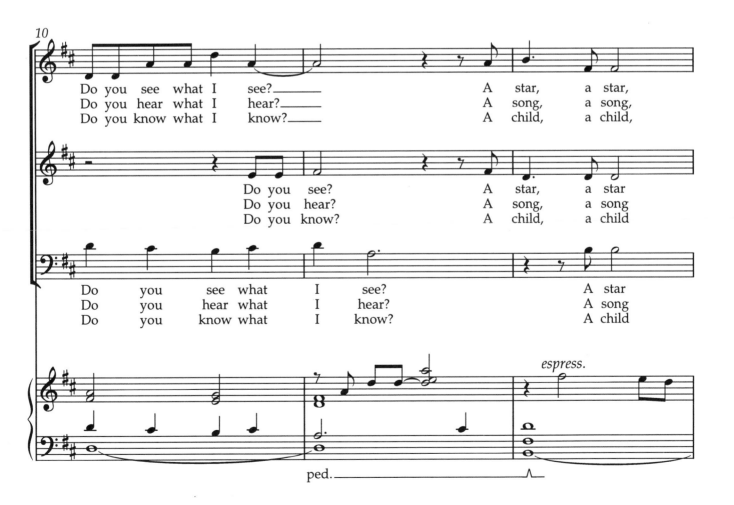

The Virgin Mary had a baby boy

Traditional
Arr. Robert Winter

wise men saw where the ba-by was born, the wise men saw where the

the ba-by was born, the wise men saw where the

The wise men saw where the

D.S. 𝄋 (p. 14) to ⊕
and then to CODA

ba-by was born___ and they saw that His name was Je - sus.

ba-by was born___ and they saw that His name was Je - sus.

ba-by was born___ and they saw that His name was Je - sus.

D.S. 𝄋 (p. 14) to ⊕
and then to CODA

⊕ CODA

glo-ri-ous, glo-ri - ous, glo-ri-ous king-dom.

glo-ri-ous, glo-ri - ous, glo-ri-ous king-dom.

glo-ri-ous, glo-ri - ous, glo-ri-ous king-dom.

⊕ CODA

Slade's smash hit *Merry Christmas, everybody* is teamed up here with *The Virgin Mary had a baby boy* and the ever-popular *Do you hear what I hear?*, in irresistible arrangements guaranteed to make your Christmas concert go off with a bang!

The *Faber Young Voices* series is devised specifically to address the needs of young or newly-formed choirs looking for easy, yet rewarding new repertoire. Each volume offers:

🍂 A coherent group of pieces to help with concert planning

🍂 Arrangements or original pieces for soprano and alto voices with a manageable piano accompaniment

🍂 An *optional* third line with a narrow range for 'baritone' (newly-changed or unstable voices) or low alto

🍂 Excellent value for money

The series spans the fullest possible range of repertoire – both traditional and popular new material from folksongs, spirituals and calypsos to show songs and Christmas favourites.

🍂 Faber Young Voices – the choral series for young choirs!

Broadway Classics *arranged by Gwyn Arch* ISBN 0-571-51660-2
Christmas Fare *Jane Sebba* ISBN 0-571-51693-9
Classic Pop Ballads *arranged by Gwyn Arch* ISBN 0-571-51639-4
Favourites from Cats *Andrew Lloyd Webber* ISBN 0-571-51614-9
Folksongs from the Wild West *arranged by Gwyn Arch* ISBN 0-571-51533-9
Four Jazz Spirituals *arranged by Gwyn Arch* ISBN 0-571-51523-1
Get on Board! *arranged by Gwyn Arch* ISBN 0-571-51609-2
The Girl from Ipanema *arranged by Gwyn Arch* ISBN 0-571-51850-8
Gospel Rock *arranged by Gwyn Arch* ISBN 0-571-51638-6
Hits from 'Oklahoma' & 'The King & I' *Rodgers & Hammerstein* ISBN 0-571-51745-5
Hits from 'South Pacific' & 'Carousel' *Rodgers & Hammerstein* ISBN 0-571-51746-3
Metropolis *Lin Marsh* ISBN 0-571-52016-2
Pat-a-Pan *arranged by Gwyn Arch* ISBN 0-571-51691-2
Smash Hits for Christmas! *arranged by Gwyn Arch & Robert Winter* ISBN 0-571-51692-0
Songs of the City *arranged by Gwyn Arch* ISBN 0-571-51799-4
Three Caribbean Calypsos *arranged by Peter Gritton* ISBN 0-571-51527-4
Tropical Daydreams *Jane Sebba* ISBN 0-571-51865-6
Walking in the Air & other seasonal songs *Howard Blake* ISBN 0-571-58047-5
West End Showstoppers *arranged by Gwyn Arch* ISBN 0-571-51679-3

FABER MUSIC · 3 QUEEN SQUARE · LONDON   www.fabermusic.com

ISBN 0-571-51692-0

9 780571 516926